HUNTING WITH POINTING DOGS

by Joe Stetson

Published by T.F.H. Publications, Inc., T.F.H. Building, 245 Cornelison Avenue, Jersey City, N. J. 07302. Distributed in the British Empire by T.F.H. Publications (London) Ltd., 13 Nutley Lane, Reigate, Surrey, England. In Canada by Clarke, Irwin & Company Ltd., Clarwin House, 791 St. Clair Avenue West, Toronto 10, Ontario, Canada. Printed in the U.S.A. by the lithograph process by T.F.H. Lithograph Corp., Jersey City, N. J. 07302.

Distributed to the Book Trade in the U.S.A. by Crown Publishers, Inc., 419 Park Avenue South, New York, N. Y. 10016.

Cover Photo by Hans Peter

Frontispiece: Mary Montrose, a great Pointer.

©1965 by T.F.H. Publications, Inc., P.O. Box 33, Jersey City, N. J. 07303

Contents

CHAPTER I. PURPOSE AND DESCRIPTION.   4
    What is a Pointing Dog? . . . What Game is Hunted With a Pointing Dog? . . . How Does a Pointing Dog Hunt?

CHAPTER II. TERMINOLOGY.   8
    Introduction to Terminology . . . Terminology.

CHAPTER III. THE NEW DOG.   14
    Obtaining the Dog . . . Naming the Puppy . . . Introducing a New Dog to the Family.

CHAPTER IV. THE FAMILY CAR.   19
    Introduction to the Car . . . Car Caution.

CHAPTER V. BASIC TRAINING.   22
    General Thoughts on Training . . . What is Expected of Dogs By Age? . . . Yard Breaking . . . Collar and Lead . . . Heeling . . . Standing . . . Recall.

CHAPTER VI. TRAINING TO RETRIEVE.   30
    Retrieving . . . Cure for Hard Mouth . . . Cure for Freezing . . . Reluctant Deliveries . . . Force Training to Retrieve.

CHAPTER VII. POINTING.   36
    Direction Signals . . . Developing the Point . . . Introduction to the Gun . . . Gunshyness . . . Steadying to Wing and Shot . . . When to Steady . . . How to Steady . . . Teaching a Dog to Back . . . Pattern . . . Adjusting Pattern.

CHAPTER VIII. CORRECTING POINTING FAULTS.   46
    Correcting the Bolter . . . Correcting the Blinker . . . Correcting the False Pointer . . . The Cure For Bumping.

CHAPTER IX. THE HUNT.   50
    Finished Control . . . Ideal Shooting Dog . . . Courtesy in the Field . . . Male or Female . . . Self Hunting.

CHAPTER X. SOME FINAL THOUGHTS.   60
    Hunting Dogs as Pets . . . Conclusion.

1. Purpose and Description

WHAT IS A POINTING DOG?

All dogs may have the instinct to point, or "freeze," even though for but an instant, upon encountering game. This is the natural pause, upon recognition of the presence of game by scent or sight, that precedes the preparation to capture it. This pointing instinct is stronger in some dogs than in others. Man has intensified this pointing characteristic by selective breeding for his own use, resulting in the production of the pointing breeds.

Better known among them are the English Setter and Pointer, the Irish and Gordon Setters, the German Shorthaired and Wirehaired Pointers, the Weimaraner, the Wirehaired Pointing Griffon, and the Brittany Spaniel; the last, of all dogs called spaniels, is the only one bred to point. Lesser

The Brittany Spaniel is the only member of the spaniel family that points game in the manner of a setter. He has been eagerly taken up by those who want a smaller pointer, and he has proved himself a fine field dog.

The bench type English Setter is, in contrast to the field dog, very showy and elegant. Bench dogs have been used successfully in the field, but generally he is not as good a hunter as the field dog.

In the United States the English Setter is divided into a field type, such as the dog above, or the bench type. The field type is very popular with American hunters for his speed, his intelligence and his wonderful intensity on point.

known are the Pudel Pointer, the more recently imported Hungarian Viszla, the Braque d' Auvergne from France, the Swedish Pointer, the German Longhaired Pointer, and the Italian Spinoni.

It must be remembered that any dog of any breeding may have sufficient instinct to point to be hunted as a pointing dog. I have known Labrador Retrievers, Airedale Terriers, and cross-breds that were excellent pointing dogs.

WHAT GAME IS HUNTED WITH A POINTING DOG?

Upland game, generally described as game that inhabits dry land, fields, orchards, and hillsides, is fair game for the pointing dog. This includes native birds such as the ruffed grouse (often partridge in the Northeast), woodcock, a meandering migrant of the snipe family, bobwhite, Gambel and California quail (called partridge in the South), and the imports: chukar partridge and the varieties of Chinese pheasant which thrive in certain sections of the country.

Rail, upland planes, and snipe are sometimes hunted with pointing dogs, and those that retrieve can double in waterfowl shooting as well. In Europe, fur as well as feather is included in a pointing dog's field of accomplishment.

The Pointer is one of the most popular gun dogs with American sportsmen. His speed, handsome appearance, intelligence and birdiness all contribute to the wide favor he enjoys. Photo by Three Lions.

The German Shorthaired Pointer has a high order of intelligence and has been used with good results on both furred and feathered game.

HOW DOES A POINTING DOG HUNT?

Bird dogs are classified generally as pointing dogs, flushing dogs, or retrievers (non-slip).

Pointing dogs work, preferably in a forward pattern, beyond the range of the gun, which is roughly thirty-five yards, seeking game in likely places. When they locate it they point and hold the point until the gun arrives, flushes the game, and shoots it. The dog may then, if he has been so trained, retrieve the game upon command. Such retrieves may be over land or water.

The great difference between the pointing dog and the flushing spaniel is obviously the fact that the former points upon encountering birds and awaits the gunner, whereas the flushing spaniel flushes boldly, immediately upon contact, making it necessary that the flush be within gun range to be effective. The greater range allowed the pointing dog, therefore, increases his potential where game is widely scattered and large areas must be searched to fill the game bag. He also may be hunted from horseback if desired. Hunting flushing dogs require that the dog's pattern and rate of travel be coordinated with the gun at all times; if it isn't, a fruitless flush-out-of-range may result.

2. Terminology

INTRODUCTION TO TERMINOLOGY

Terms and expressions traditionally used in reference to a subject are often explained in an appendix. The reader, therefore, should he encounter a term which he may well have heard but the meaning of which is not perhaps clear or comprehensive, must read the text and then refer to the appendix for clarification. It seems more logical to come to an understanding regarding terms associated with pointing dogs at the outset of our discussion. We can then be sure that the reader and writer have similar interpretations. Confusion will be avoided and time saved.

TERMINOLOGY

BACKCAST is a swing in the opposite direction from the progress of the hunt which results in the dog's coming up from behind.

BACKING is the action of a dog coming to a stop upon seeing another dog on point or upon the command of the handler who sees the other dog's situation. This is called sight backing or backing on command.

BLINKING is backing from, circumventing, or otherwise leaving game after becoming aware of it. Blinking is a serious fault, usually resulting from a dog's fear of punishment should the bird be flushed. A very sensitive dog may even be afraid of the exposive flush of a bird or shy of the gunshot that usually follows a flush.

BODY SCENT is the scent direct from the body of a bird.

BOLTING is taking off, ceasing to hunt to the gun. A dog may do this to demonstrate his scorn of the handler or to escape the discipline he is undergoing.

BREAKING refers to either (1) chasing a flushed bird or moving on or retrieving before the command to move on or retrieve has been given or (2) training generally or specifically to be steady to wing and shot.

BUMPING is flushing a bird that should have been located and pointed.

CAST is the swing a dog takes in quartering his territory.

CAST OFF is the releasing of a dog at the start of a hunt or at the "breakaway," or beginning, of the contest between the two dogs of a brace at a field trial.

CHECKING is confirming the position and progress of the handler, usually as one cast is being completed or one piece of cover negotiated before proceeding to the next.

The breakaway at a field trial.

CORRECTION is the independent re-evaluation of the conditions after a flash or short point, and moving on. Usually a bird has been in the area and left.

DIVIDED POINT is the situation occurring when two or more dogs encounter game and point, each independent of the other and unaware of the other's point.

FALL refers to the shot bird, whether killed or crippled, and the spot at which it came to earth.

FALSE POINTING is, as implied, pointing when the game is not there. It can be when the game has been there, when there have been lesser birds present, or even when there is nothing to point. Some dogs learn that they can stop and rest or get special attention from the handler if they adopt a pointing attitude.

FLAGGING is moving the tail while on point, which is an indication of lack of intensity or that the game has moved out from under the point.

FLASH POINT is a momentary point expected of young pointing dogs before they develop the intensity and training to hold indefinitely.

FREEZING is holding a retrieve, that is, failing to give it up freely and resisting attempts by the handler to take it.

GROUND SCENT is the scent left by game on the ground or bushes, weeds and grasses as it moves about through them.

Although pointing dogs are not water workers by nature, it is important for the dog to be able to make water retrieves. Many upland game birds are shot over water, and the dog should be able to recover them.

Hunting with dogs is worthwhile from the conservation point of view, since a cripple will not get away from a dog, leaving strong birds in the field.

HACKING is overhandling by giving repeated commands, usually of a type that inhibit a dog's work instead of leaving him to his own initiative.

HARD MOUTH is obviously the type of carry that renders a bird more fit for dog food than for the table.

HEAD TRAILING is a more subtle method of trailing in which a dog runs ahead of his bracemate while watching out of the corner of his eye for the bracemate's change of direction and changing direction accordingly. A casual observer might think the wrong dog is trailing.

MAKING GAME is showing signs of becoming aware of the presence of game. This is indicated when a dog's tail action accelerates, his interest seems to multiply, his straight running drops to a slower and more quartering pattern, and his actions seem searching and cautious. This usually ends in a point, an accidental flush and automatic stop to flush, a flush and chase, or the search proving fruitless and the dog moving on at the previous rate and style.

MARKING is noting the location of a fall and remembering it until the bird is retrieved from that location or, should it be a runner, trailed from the fall and retrieved.

POINTING is the cessation of motion and becoming muscularly intense, regardless of position, upon encountering the scent or sight of game.

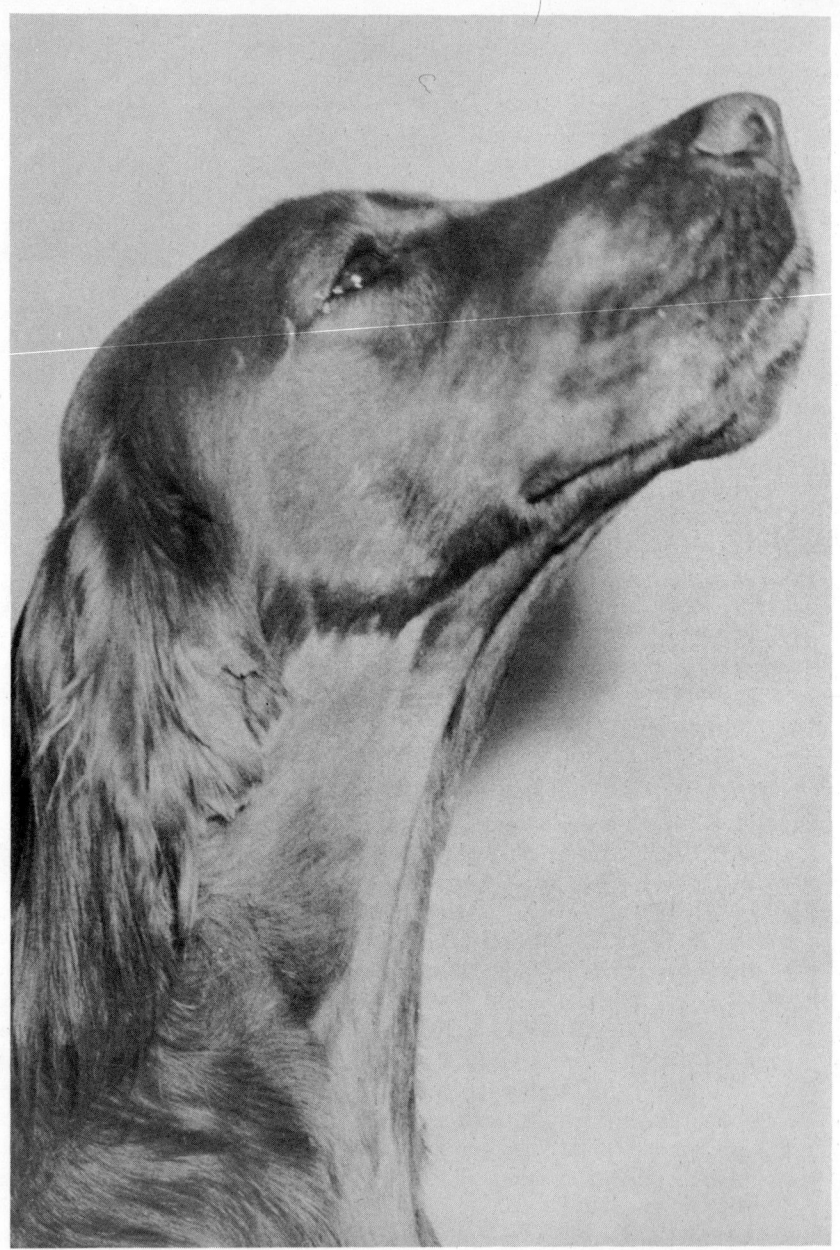

The Irish Setter is one of the most handsome of all breeds. For a long time the breed was bred for appearance to such an extent that hunting ability was greatly dimmed. Field interest in the Irish Setter is now on the upswing, and the future of the red Irishman as a field dog seems assured.

POINT STEALING is moving in, usually closer than a dog that has already established a point, while being obviously aware of that dog's situation.

ROADING is exercising a dog for conditioning, usually on a road and by car or horseback. Not to be confused with:

ROADING UP OR IN is moving up cautiously to establish a positive point after being stopped temporarily by a faint or indefinite scent of game.

SOFTENING (sometimes accompanied by going down, settling, or squatting) is losing intensity on point. This may occur coincidentally with flagging, but more often as the game moves on or is flushed. Also it may be an indication that a dog is reacting to such reprimand or punishment as was used in breaking. (German-trained dogs are trained to drop on flush as a protection during the multiple shooting that follows the flush in the continental method of bird harvesting.)

STAUNCH, or STANCH, is the quality of remaining on point as originally established until the arrival of the gun.

STEADY TO WING AND SHOT is to remain in the original position of the point after the flush or the shot respectively. (Some dogs will break upon flush, others upon hearing the shot or seeing the bird fall.)

STOP TO FLUSH is stopping by command, or preferably of the dog's own initiative, until commanded to go on, when a bird is accidentally or inadvertently flushed.

TRAILING is the habit some dogs have of following a bracemate with no regard for hunting independently.

UNPRODUCTIVE is a situation in which game cannot be produced after a positive point.

3. The New Dog

OBTAINING THE DOG

For those who have yet to get a dog, a few words based upon experience will not be out of place. Price is not the sole consideration. Many a good dog has been purchased for a low figure. When a good prospect may be had for a high figure, however, it may still be a bargain; the lifetime cost of a dog is what should be considered, and a poor specimen is no bargain no matter how low the price. Make sure the quality is there and the source is reliable. Be certain, too, that the prospect has a good, bold temperament, without which all other qualities will be at a disadvantage. Only a healthy, fearless puppy can be expected to take to conventional training methods and be happy working with you.

A good field dog will often show indications of his ability while still very young. This four-month-old German Shorthaired Pointer executes a take-off just like that of an adult dog.

Puppies should be allowed to investigate their surroundings frequently. This comes naturally to them and will help in later training.

The best gun dogs are bred from field stock. Each puppy represents a great deal of planning and effort on the part of his breeder.

A good way to decide the breed of dog you wish to buy is to look them all over for appearance at a dog show. But, by all means, be sure your hunting prospect comes from hunting stock. Watching dogs work at a field trial or accompanying a friend afield with his dogs or asking a breeder to run a prospect or two for you to see their "way-of-going" and desire to hunt will demonstrate more of the qualities you must have.

NAMING THE PUPPY

Many puppies go to their new owners with completed registrations or with recommended names which identify the breeder and the bloodlines, but no one is going to feel comfortable or effective yelling, "here Eveready," because his pup's registered name is Woodland's Eveready. Call names should be carefully chosen at the beginning and used consistently thereafter. Choose a name that sounds neither like that of any member of the family (canine, feline, or otherwise) nor similar to any of the usual commands. Make it short and distinctive—different if possible. Common call names are Rip, Jake, Tom, Ike, and Belle. You can come up with one that may describe the dog as well as carry clearly and involve no confusion. Just remember the common commands are "come," "down," "sit," "whoa," "fetch," "hie on," "come round," "leave it," and any others you may wish to put to use. It is obvious that Joe and "whoa," Clown and "down," and Brian and "hie on" could be confusing.

These Vizsla puppies are reluctant to leave their mother. In a short time, however, they will be on the way to becoming self-reliant, first class shooting dogs.

The production of good field dogs is a costly venture. Breeders devote a great deal of time, money and effort to producing a good litter. Sportsmen who buy puppies of this sort are sure to make a wise investment.

STARTING TO TRAIN

The mistake most often made is starting advanced training too early. We are too likely to accept the pup's intelligence as being equal to our own or to a human child's. Remember, not only is the canine intelligence much more limited but also a pup is running around much earlier in its mental development than a human child, granting, of course, that such potential as it does acquire comes at a more rapid rate.

A great deal of harm has resulted from recent research which determined that a puppy's threshold of awareness began at about six weeks of age. Interpreting this as meaning that this is the time for intense training is a gross error. A great deal can be accomplished with a puppy at this tender age, but more in terms of confidence, an understanding tone of voice, the meaning of *yes* and *no*, *do* and *don't*, than in terms of specific performance. It is then that trust and companionship and mutual understanding can be welded or insecurity and unresponsiveness be produced by rough treatment, inconsistency, confusion, or neglect.

17

From three months of age onward a pup can be taken afield. Don't be concerned about the flash points at butterflies or sparrows that are so often made much of. They can be topics of dramatic conversation, but there is little connection between these baby reactions and real pointing that may develop from six months of age upward. I have known youngsters that put on a great show with grasshoppers at six weeks that wouldn't point a grouse at six years.

It is important that young dogs get plenty of experience in hunting cover, but it is equally important that exercise be controlled until they are mature and conditioned so that they do not overexert. Dogs of any age must be exercised with discretion in hot weather.

INTRODUCING A NEW DOG TO THE FAMILY

When a dog is first brought into the home, the entire family should be instructed in advance so that the new arrival will feel as comfortable as possible. Let a new dog make his own advances. Keep voices down and actions quiet. Don't let any member of the family descend upon the dog or puppy to pet or hug it no matter how well intentioned the gesture. The dog will soon become friendly to some member of the family circle, and I'll wager it won't be the one who snaps his fingers and slaps his thigh.

4. The Family Car

INTRODUCTION TO THE CAR

Transportation by automobile has become so important to modern living that a dog that dislikes it or become carsick can be burdensome.

It is best to be prepared for carsickness by not feeding a dog before its first experiences in car transport. This will minimize the inconvenience should the dog upchuck as puppies often will on their first ride. (It has been my experience that tiny puppies, of an age when they are not too conscious of their surroundings, rarely become sick when transported.) Be prepared with newspaper and cleaning cloths in case of an accident.

What is the best cure for carsickness? In my opinion carsickness is caused by nervousness, and I have never found a case that did not respond favorably to repeated short trips—always keeping the dog happy and feeding it each time it returned. Extended trips can soon be made successfully.

An energetic take-off, such as this one, thrills the heart of any gun dog enthusiast.

CAR CAUTION

There are several precautionary measures which should be carefully observed when transporting dogs by car:

Never leave a dog in a car in the sun with the windows closed. This has caused the death or blindness of many a dog resulting from sustained high temperature.

Use care in closing doors. Careless slamming of car doors has broken many a tail or injured a foot or ear.

Never transport a loaded gun in a car with or without a dog. The presence of a dog to trigger the gun increases the hazard.

It is inadvisable to allow a dog to ride with his head sticking out of the car window. Dogs' eyes were not meant to be exposed to winds at modern highway speeds. Dogs, moreover, have been known to jump out of moving cars, and an emergency stop or swerve may cause a dog to fall out.

Don't transport a dog in a car trunk unless it is properly ventilated by air vents designed to get air from the front. Propping open the trunk lid is

Dogs should not be permitted to endanger themselves by putting their heads out of a window in a moving car. Photo by Percy Jones.

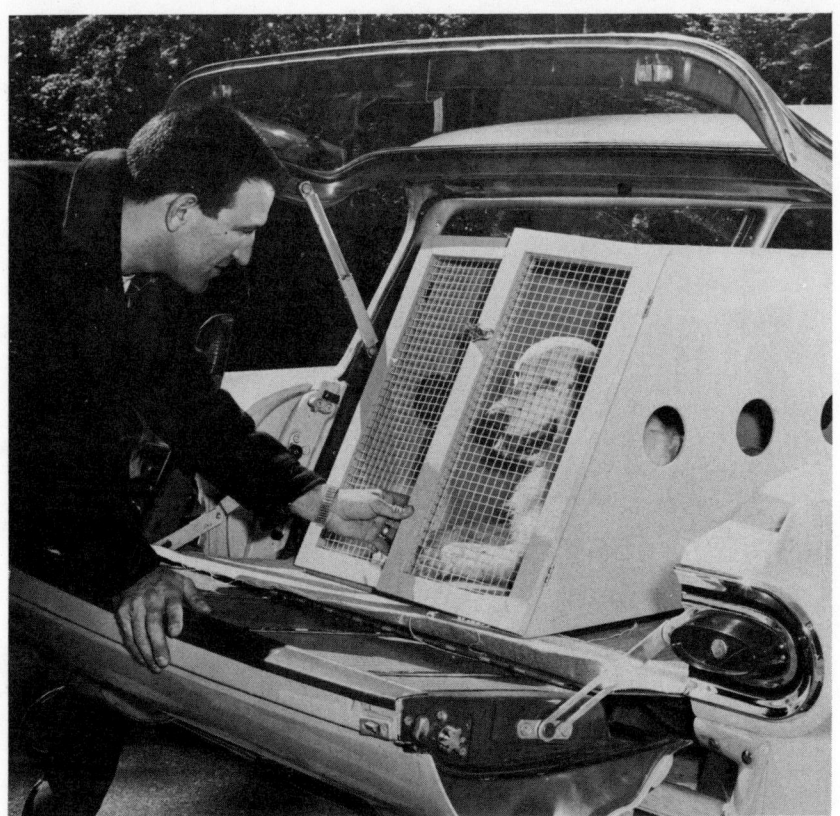

The best way to transport dogs is in traveling crates. They arrive in the hunting field in good spirits and have not been jostled about during the ride.

worse than keeping it closed. This increases the flow of carbon monoxide—contaminated exhaust gases. Dogs are several times as susceptible to carbon monoxide as humans, and expecting a dog to make best use of his scenting powers after exposure to exhaust gases is a bit ridiculous.

The ideal method for protecting dog, car, and driver is to install a crate within the car which will contain the dog comfortably at all times, especially when he is tired, wet, muddy, and bur-entangled after a hunt.

Lastly, train your dog to sit or stand quietly until given the command to enter or leave the car. Confusion often results from a dog bolting into a car the moment the door is open. Many a dog has been injured or killed by slipping out of a car door before the owner was ready to restrain or protect him properly. In fact, many a hunt has been delayed until a poorly disciplined dog has been located and retrieved by the hunting party. The control starts right at the car.

5. Basic Training

GENERAL THOUGHTS ON TRAINING

Training periods should be frequent, but of short duration. The span of attention of a dog, particularly at puppy age, is only a few minutes. It is best to stop a training session while the pupil is *still enthusiastic*.

Don't train in the presence of other dogs or people until the lesson has been well learned. It is then a good idea to introduce diversions slowly so that the performance is perfected under all conditions.

Let the pupil run off excess steam before endeavoring to control for teaching. This is much better than fighting the excess enthusiasm and having to apply undue pressure. End the session when there is still enthusiasm enough for a friendly romp.

Most English Setters used in the field are derived from the Llewelyn strain. In modern times, though, there are no true separate strains of the English Setter. Photo by Bob Horowitz.

These puppies have been taught control by waiting quietly for food. This training will come in handy when they are taught steadiness on point.

Pointing dogs work by means of a specific pattern, incorporating the quartering of a field and coming to a staunch point when the bird is located.

Be consistent and follow through. Don't give a command unless you expect to see it obeyed or are willing to make the effort to enforce it. See that others associated with the dog are instructed and prepared to do the same.

Never train or reprimand in anger; never reprimand unless the dog is in the act of disobeying. Unless the reprimand is associated with the deed it can bring no result but confusion.

Train in a soft voice and with a modulated whistle. If a dog is shouted at in training it will logically expect such commands all its life. After training, continue to handle with modulated commands. A frustrated voice or an overblown whistle are soon recognized by a smart dog as an indication of frustration: a sign that the handler has reached the end of his rope and can do nothing about it. The dog then is on his own beyond the handler's reach and knows it.

Consistency in commands is also important and commands should not overlap. *"Charge," "get down,"* and *"lie down"* can all be covered by *"down."* To say *"sit down,"* then, is overlapping. *"Sit"* is sufficient and less confusing. *"Here"* is a superflous addition to *"come."* In a pointing dog, *"whoa"* will take care of *"stand"* or *"stay."*

The dog on the right has located and is pointing the game. The dog on the left is honoring the point of the other. These two English Setters represent the ideal in gun dog training.

Mr. and Mrs. G. H. Ryman have bred English Setters that are capable of good performance in the hunting field and are handsome enough to do well in the show ring.

WHAT IS EXPECTED OF DOGS BY AGE?

From three to nine months of age a pup should have a growing enthusiasm for hunting. Its span of attention and application to hunting in likely places should increase with age, and flash points may be expected during this time. Yard training can be begun at six months and by nine months a puppy should be walking at heel, and coming and downing on command. Retrieving may be natural by this time, though not necessarily finished in performance.

By a year or fifteen months of age most pointing breeds should be pointing. Continental breeds may even be backing and steady to wing and shot by fifteen months. Attaining these levels at the ages mentioned or earlier is good practice only if it is done without loss of enthusiasm, drive, and range.

YARD BREAKING

Yard training is not only usually more convenient but also it enables the handler to forge the elements of control without dulling the edge of the dog's desire to hunt as might result from reprimanding while working the dog on birds or in bird country. It starts with accustoming a pup to a collar and ends with finished retrieving which might include direction signals.

The Wirehaired Pointing Griffon is an old breed but is not popular in the United States. American hunters desire a dog that is faster on the move than the Griffon is. He is, though, a first class gun dog, as those who have shot over him will attest. Photo by Evelyn Shafer.

COLLAR AND LEAD

Put a collar on your pup for a day or two before attaching a lead, then let him drag the lead around for a few minutes at a time for a few days (never leave him alone to get hung up and possibly strangle himself to death).

HEELING

It is customary to have the dog on the handler's left side. Now take the end of the lead and walk out saying *"heel"* and patting the side of your left thigh. The puppy will probably walk along with you, though a bit slower or faster or at a tangent. If he lags behind, jerk (don't pull) lightly on the lead and repeat *"heel."* Leave the lead slack as much as possible and praise the puppy when he is doing well. Repeat *"heel"* and jerk in the corrective direction whenever necessary to improve performance. In time the puppy will learn that it is much pleasanter to walk at heel and will do so. When the youngster is performing consistently on lead, including right and left turns and reasonable changes of speed, try heeling off lead. Remember that nothing helps quite so much as praise in a pleasant tone of voice when the puppy is doing well.

STANDING

When your puppy has begun to get the idea of walking at heel on lead, say *"whoa"* each time you come to a stop. In usual obedience training procedure dogs are trained to sit each time the handler comes to a stop. In training pointing dogs I recommend that the dog stop in a standing position for the following reasons: first, it takes more time to sit; second, sitting a large dog, especially one with a long coat in wet, muddy weather means more dirt in the house or car; third, any training to sit may cause the dog to go down (get soft or lose loftiness) on point because of association with training; and fourth, and perhaps the most important, teaching the dog to whoa can be much simpler if started right at this stage. After the dog has been heeling off lead and stand-stopping, repeat *"whoa"* and walk away from him, repeating the command and thrusting the palm of the open hand toward him if he moves. Since he has already been stopping on the command from his lead training, this should not be difficult to accomplish.

Rakk-Selle, a Vizsla, displays a perfect point, which is a prerequisite for any pointer or setter.

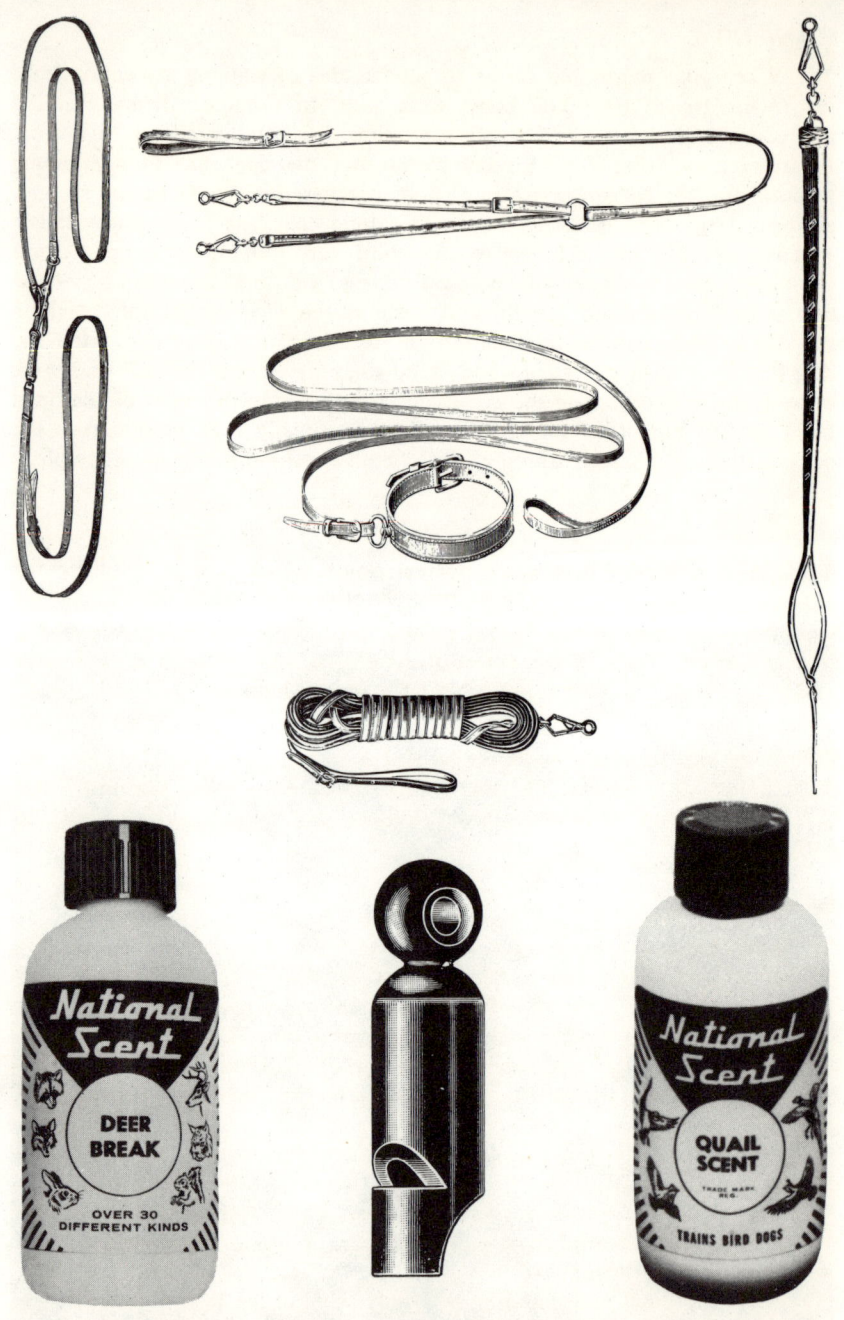

These are some of the supplies needed in the training and working with all pointing dogs.

War Storm, winner of the Purina trophy, represents the culmination of a trainer's effort. It is a great accomplishment to start off with a youngster and make a top field dog of him.

Return to him promptly with praise and a pat at first, then lengthen the periods until he is steady. The dog should never come when you fail to let him know by your manner or tone of voice that he pleases you when he performs well.

RECALL

Teaching a puppy to come on command may result from the puppy's natural pleasure and desire to be with you. This same desire, however, may be supplemented by some stronger desire to pursue some other course when he is afield and begins to develop a mind of his own. Unless a dog's sense of obedience to a recall command by voice or whistle is consistent and strong, therefore, it is best to use the simple force method generally accepted by trainers.

Fasten a twenty-foot piece of light line to the dog's collar. Whoa the dog, then walk away to the full extent of the line. Give the command to come and bring the line in rapidly hand over hand. Repeat until the pupil responds freely. Remember the importance of praise, consistency, and frequent but short sessions.

When the pupil is responding promptly without the line, a long inviting whistle can be gradually substituted for the voice command. (Retrievers are traditionally recalled with one long and two short trills.)

6. Training to Retrieve

RETRIEVING

Many pups just naturally carry objects about. If you take an object and throw it a short distance, your puppy can't bring it back too fast or too often. Such a natural retriever may perform consistently and reliably all its life. Many times, however, the joyful retriever does a great job just so long as he is having a ball. When the chips are down and a retrieve is particularly difficult or in some way different from the fun he has been having, he may decide it is no longer fun and leave you in the lurch. If your dog seems to be developing well as a natural retriever, it is logical to polish up his natural inclinations until the time comes when it is obvious that force training is called for.

There are a few "don'ts" for the trainer whose natural prospect may seem to be sailing along in fine shape. Never use a hard object for a retrieve. It may be a hazard to the dog's teeth, and it certainly will encourage a hard mouth since a dog must clamp down harder on hard objects than on soft ones which can practically hang in the mouth by the small indentations made by the teeth when held gently. Don't throw objects to be caught. Soon, youngsters will be throwing stones for the dog to catch. Never send a dog for a retrieve which does not exist. You cannot expect to trust him if he cannot trust you.

When your dog is retrieving well, insist that he whoa until he has been commanded to fetch. This steadying is not recommended until a dog is at least nine months old. If it seems to take the edge off the dog's enthusiasm for retrieving, proceed with caution.

An old cloth twisted and knotted can be worked with on land. A small boat bumper is very practical for land and water work, and such bumpers are used extensively for training. Feathers are often tied to an artificial "retrieve" (retrieving buck, or buck) to accustom the dog to feathers and aid the transition to birds. Scents used on retrieving bucks aid this transition and will speed the training. They may be obtained in your sporting goods store. They certainly increase the amount of scent rising from a buck and aid in its location on a difficult retrieve. Scents for quail, pheasant, and duck are readily available.

When a dog is retrieving well—remaining steady to command, marking the fall accurately, picking up promptly, carrying with a soft mouth, and delivering willingly to hand—you need only require the dog to set and offer the bird to hand in order to polish off the performance.

This Weimaraner is executing a perfect retrieve and delivering the bird to hand. Proper training has avoided establishment of retrieving faults in this dog. Photo by Evelyn Shafer.

CURE FOR HARD MOUTH

Clamping down on a bird or chomping it while retrieving is cured by a simple device, for which I know no better substitute. Get a few finishing nails of a length equal to the diameter of the buck. Drive them through the buck in different directions. If the dog clamps down on a buck so prepared it is obvious that he will find it uncomfortable. A soft delivery can be made with no distress to him whatsoever.

CURE FOR FREEZING

After many years of consideration, I am convinced that freezing is merely an endeavor on the dog's part to retain contact with the handler. By making the delivery, the dog-man relationship will be over; therefore, the dog hangs on to the bird in order to prolong it. The solution is to throw out a short retrieve just as the dog is about to deliver. Thus he will feel that there is more to be done and will deliver. As he makes the second (and much shorter retrieve) throw out a third. The dog will usually get the feeling that these short retrieves will continue indefinitely and will stop freezing.

The Weimaraner has earned the name of "Gray Ghost." His striking color and appearance have been responsible for this as well as the confident and commanding way he covers the hunting field. Photo by Louise Van der Meid.

Hess Von Schloos Loosdorf, a Vizsla, owned by Dr. I. S. Osborn, shows his hunting skill on a take-off. The Vizsla is catching on fast with American hunters.

RELUCTANT DELIVERIES

When a dog retrieves well with the exception of the final few feet, it is usually for the same reason that a dog freezes: he doesn't wish to end the game. To encourage a prompt delivery, back up a few steps as the dog approaches. He will usually feel that you are leaving and will hasten the retrieve. If the response isn't enough, turn and walk away. He will not want to be left behind.

FORCE TRAINING TO RETRIEVE

If you decide that your dog should be or must be force trained to retrieve, it is best to wait until he is mature and free from all other major field problems.

Put the pupil on lead. Open his mouth and put the retrieving buck in it. Close his mouth and tap him under the chin lightly to keep his head up and his lower jaw closed. He will probably try to drop the buck, but do not let him. Tap his lower jaw and head up each time he tries. Praise him while he holds.

Keeping his head up, heel the dog about on lead. When he has walked about holding the buck, command *"give"* while taking the buck with the hand, approaching from beneath with palm up. Praise him for the carry and delivery. Repeat this as often as practical until he carries the buck about dependably.

The ringneck pheasant is a strong bird. Care should be taken so that the young dog is not spurred or startled by one. This may cause him to develop into a blinker. Photo by Morley Baer.

The German breeders developed the Weimaraner to be an all-around dog. He is as at home in the water as he is working on land. Photo by Louise Van der Meid.

Now drop the buck on the ground in front of the dog. His head will probably bob downward to investigate. Take advantage of this by holding his head down and bringing the buck up to it while saying *"fetch."* Repeat until the dog will pick the buck up from the ground.

You are now ready to throw the buck a short distance while keeping the dog steady (he has either already been taught to whoa or can now be trained to retrieve only after your command). Give the command *"fetch,"* and lead him to the buck. Insist upon his picking it up; then lead him back to the start. Do this repeatedly and for longer distances until you are ready to try him off lead. Since each step has been done by force, the inclination to do only that which he wishes will be absent and the reliability of his performance will be greater than that of most natural retrievers. Polishing up mouth, delivery, marking, and pick-up can follow.

7. Pointing

DIRECTION SIGNALS

Many pointing dogs, including quail pointers, may never be required to retrieve or, certainly, to take direction signals, but the versatility and usefulness of the multiple-purpose dog, which you may wish to use for varied game, will be greatly increased if you add the mastery of direction signals to his other accomplishments.

It is of prime importance that signals be properly given. Stepping to the right or left while swinging the respective arm in that direction and holding it out until the dog responds to it takes care of "right" and "left." The recall brings a dog in, and an overhead arm sends the dog deeper into the field.

The Pointer's speed and stamina enable him to quarter a field and find birds in an efficient fashion. His great popularity among field dog men has not come to him for no reason.

The Vizsla is as intense on point as his English counterpart. The practice of docking the tail tip is so that the end of the tail will not be slashed by thorns in the hunting field.

To get response to the left signal, throw a second retrieving buck to the left as the dog is returning with the first. When he has made the delivery, give the left signal. Do this repeatedly, then work to the right. When he does both well in sequence, mix them up. By showing him the retrieve to left or right, then following with the proper arm movement, he will soon recognize that there should be a retrieve to the left when you swing your arm in that direction and so on. You can then throw a buck over his head as he is returning and get the idea of a deeper retrieve to associate with the signal to go deeper on *"get back,"* as the retriever handlers command with the overhead arm signal.

DEVELOPING THE POINT

Assisting a dog to establish a firm point may precede retriever training. In fact it would do so of necessity if it is not intended that a dog retrieve.

It is, of course, hoped that a prospect will have at least the instinct to flash point. It is further hoped that a dog, as it matures, will hold a point long enough for the handler to get to it. If the handler sees the dog making game, he can be prepared for the flash point and command *"whoa."* This should enable the handler to get to the dog and "style it up."

Ch. Red Echo of Ardee, owned by Harry Dean. This Irish Setter is an example of the field and bench winner, a credit to any sporting breed.

Raising the dog's tail and elevating its position, if there is a tendency to settle, will improve the dog's appearance on point, and pushing it gently forward will increase its intensity and firm it up. After pushing gently and whoaing softly and encouragingly for a few moments, flush the game, and, by all means, let the dog chase it. Only by finding, pointing, and chasing is the dog going to build up the enthusiasm necessary to carry on with zest from one game contact to another. Enjoy the dog's exuberance and cheer his chasing on in your heart, because only the dog that finds and chases with all the energy at his command is going to be worth the trouble of molding into a finished dog.

INTRODUCTION TO THE GUN

Gunshyness is as discouraging as any fault a hunting dog may have. It may prove quite difficult to cure. It is important, therefore, to take every precaution in respect to gun shot until it is proven that the dog has no fear of it. The procedure may be quite unnecessary, but failure to follow a careful course may be disastrous.

Wait until the prospect is of an age and condition that you would call robust. Take the dog afield and hunt him until he finds birds. He will be flushing and chasing wildly at this stage and enjoying every bit of it. Every trainer should carry a .22 blank pistol. When the dog is in the liveliest part of a chase-after-flush, and you are at a distance, fire the .22. Chances are a thousand to one the dog won't even notice it. Graduated shots up to the shotgun, preferably light bore, can then follow with discretion. If he does react, but not seriously, try again after a flush or two and at a greater distance. If he quits and shows signs of real shyness, one of the recommended treatments is indicated. Using a gun to condition a dog when the game is not present to absorb his interest and to build a pleasant association between game and gun may work, but it is certainly not as desirable. Many dogs have been made gunshy by mechanical attempts to harden them to the gun, only a few by accidents.

Field Ch. Allamuchy Valley Addie, a Brittany Spaniel, owned by Howard Niper. The Brittany is the only spaniel that points game. Many hunters desiring a smaller dog have found the Brittany to be "just what the doctor ordered."

GUNSHYNESS

There are two rather drastic methods often used to cure gunshyness. One is to fire a light bore gun at a distance each time the dog approaches his feed pan. If he fails to muster enough courage to eat, take away his food. Repeat this two or three times a day until the dog's hunger is stronger than his fear of the gun, to which he may be gradually accustoming himself.

The other drastic method is to take the dog aboard a safe but maneuverable boat. Shoot a light bore gun, in a direction away from the dog, of course. If he goes overboard, let him swim a while, then bring him aboard and try it again. The idea is that after sufficient fatigue from swimming, the dog will prefer to remain in the boat where he learns that the noise does him no harm. These two methods are negative in their approach and can wind up with a psychotic dog and, perhaps, a psychotic owner as well.

A better method may be costlier in birds and requires the help of a friend or two with experienced dogs. Get some birds; tie the dog and the experienced dogs in a group near a bit of low cover where the birds may be planted. Make the distance enough so the shot will not be too sharp,

Some people like to use a brace consisting of two breeds. Here an English Setter has made game and is on point, and his bracemate, a Pointer, is honoring.

This Pointer is on line and intensely awaits the command of his handler to quarter the ground.

but near enough so the dogs will be able to see the flush, flight, and fall of the planted birds. The veterans will enjoy the procedure. The gunshy dog should eventually succumb to their contagious enthusiasm. When he seems to be ready for it, release him, and let him locate a fall. Let him flush a planted bird and hope that when he flushes it your shot will not cause a recurrence of his distress. The lighter the loads used in such a procedure, the greater the chances of success.

STEADYING TO WING AND SHOT

I have heard many torrid arguments on the subject of whether or not a dog should be steady to wing and to shot. There has never been any doubt in my mind that a dog is not under control unless steady. The pleasure of gunning over a dog that is steady is infinitely greater than over one which takes off cross country with nothing on his mind but chasing a flying bird, to say nothing of the fact that such a dog cannot be hunted with a broken dog. He may flush other game out of gun range during his chase. He wastes time chasing, and, in today's limited cover, he may run across rapidly traveled highways in his pell mell pursuit. He may even jump into a shot pattern with a low flying bird. The clinching argument in my mind is that I have never found a proponent of the idea that dogs need not be steady who had a steady dog. The argument is always for broken dogs by those who have and appreciate them and against them by those whose dogs or whose efforts haven't made the grade. I cite this because the novice should beware the persuasion of the "have nots" and become "haves" themselves so they may appreciate the "complete pointing dog."

WHEN TO STEADY

When a dog has been pointing and holding sufficiently long for you to flush and kill birds over him and he is chasing with enthusiasm—having no fear of handler, flush, or gun — you may proceed to make him steady. Depending on the breed, this will usually be when the dog is between twelve and eighteen months of age. It is most important that you accomplish this with the least loss of enthusiasm. This requires careful handling and disciplining.

HOW TO STEADY

Carry a check cord while your hunting partner carries the gun. When the dog points, get to him, repeating *"whoa,"* confidently praising him at the same time. Fasten the check cord to his collar, firm up his point and have your partner flush the bird while you hold him. Repeat, but allow some leeway. If he remains steady, have your partner kill the bird and bring it back to him. If he breaks, you fetch up sharply and your partner does not shoot. More drastically, if necessary, let the line run to the end when he breaks and fetch him up sharply. You may or may not flick him with the flushing whip, depending upon the need and his reaction. Never shoot a bird over him if he breaks. He must learn that the game is bagged if he is steady and lost if he chases.

It should not be necessary for me to say that, at one time or another, a dog that has retained his spirit, will, for some reason or other, break. Don't ever let him get away with it or your efforts will go down the drain.

TEACHING A DOG TO BACK

It is not only a pleasure but also a privilege to gun over a dog with perfect manners. One requirement of such perfection is honoring another dog's point. Stealing a point, flushing the game from under another dog's point, or, because of the competitive spirit engendered by competition, causing the other dog to break and chase, all greatly reduce the pleasure of gunning over pointing dogs.

PATTERN

The pattern of a shooting dog is a controversial subject. Unfortunately, it is usually being discussed in terms of each man's own shooting areas and

The basic advantage to hunting with a dog is that the dog's keen sense of smell can overcome color camouflage. This English Setter is pointing a grouse which is so well hidden that it is almost invisible.

dogs. To express my opinion, as far as range is concerned, a well-trained dog can be handled to the range of any kind of cover; as far as geometric pattern is concerned, a dog should hunt likely objectives in a forward manner, making his casts so as to come out ahead of the gun before making his next swing. For a pointing dog to zig and zag across an open field, devoid of holding or feeding cover, is a waste of time and energy. He should travel the hedgerows, swing on the leeward side of copses of bushes and trees and the edges of swamps, investigating the locations where birds will more likely be feeding. A dog can, in this way, cover a lot of territory in a short time and increase production when birds are scarce or scattered.

"But if he's too far away in heavy cover you can't see him," is the complaint of the under-your-feet advocate. It is not necessary to see a pointing dog at all times. This is where staunchness and steadiness become invaluable assets. A handler should be able, by knowing his dog's way-of-going and observing his casts, to figure just about where he is and where he should be expected to show out front. If he doesn't appear about as expected, the handler can usually go to the area in which the dog may be on point. True, some hunters haven't the faculty for observing and calculating the dog's position without conscious effort. They will either have to develop the faculty, hack their dogs in closer, or be satisfied with dogs that have no desire to get out of spaniel range.

Ch. Rusty V. Schwarenburg, a German Shorthaired Pointer, was a top field winner in the 1940's. He is a perfect example of the versatility of his breed, being a winner on the bench as well as in the field.

The Pointer is a dog of great determination. The expression on his face and the eagerness with which he starts out show his devotion to his time-honored occupation.

ADJUSTING PATTERN

If a dog has been taught hand signals, it is a simple matter to get his attention and signal him to swing to right or left. If the dog is at a distance it may be necessary to walk a few steps in the desired direction with the arm outstretched. If you hunt on horseback, a dog soon becomes accustomed to taking the direction of the horse's head.

When a dog is ranging wider than the handler wishes, the recall whistle should bring him in to a position from which he can be given a left or right signal.

While considering pattern, I would like to mention a fault very common among novices. They somehow get the idea that a pointing dog should come all the way in to them at the end of each cast. Thus the dog is beating a path to and from the handler over ground the handler will be covering. This is a gross waste of the dog's time and energy. A check from a distance before each successive cast is all that is needed to keep dog and handler in contact.

This might be a good time to mention that a handler can lose a dog easily, despite the dog's effort to maintain contact, by making a change of direction when the dog is out of sight. The time to change is when the dog is checking and can observe the change. Otherwise, the dog can be recalled to a position from which he can observe the change in direction.

8. Correcting Pointing Faults

CORRECTING THE BOLTER

Some dogs, whether from a hard-headed streak or because they become fed up with hacking or even well-administered discipline, decide to strike out for themselves. They usually decide this when they are out far enough so they think they cannot be reached by the handler. A trainer on horseback can run such a dog down and give it a lesson in recall. A foot trainer is better off not wasting his breath or voice on whistle. Such dogs should have a long check line attached to their collars. The other end of this should be reached when they fail to respond and the recall lesson emphasized.

It is an easy matter to correct most pointing faults, but it is much better to train in such a way that faults are never established to begin with.

The Weimaraner and the German Shorthaired Pointer are both relatively new to the United States, but both have acquired faithful followings among field trial men.

CORRECTING THE BLINKER

If you are so unfortunate as to find that your dog is locating game and then either circumventing it or even backing out of a piece of cover to avoid it, you may well suspect that he is doing this from fear of the consequences if the bird is flushed. Possibly, the flush itself may disturb a sensitive dog, especially if, as a puppy, a planted pheasant flushed in his face. He may fear the shot which will follow the flush. There is greater probability that he has been punished for flushing or in the process of breaking for steadiness and he wishes to avoid trouble.

The cure must be something that will make him enjoy what he is doing. A traditional method is to kill as many birds as possible over him and praise him. It may even be necessary to let him break again, though this is a serious setback. Giving him the heads of the birds killed over him may help.

The cooperation of another dog is, of course, required to teach a dog to back or honor. Assuming that your dog stops on command, whoa him when the other dog points and your dog is in a position to be aware of it. Go up to your dog and, continuing gentle "whoa talk," improve his stance, if necessary, as you did when you were just styling him up on point. If your dog is not inclined to whoa because of the competitive circumstances, let him run with a check cord so you can get to him at the right moment. If your dog cannot see the other dog's situation from where he is working, call him over and whoa him and get to the check cord if necessary.

It is natural for dogs to have some instinct to back—some or enough so they never need special training. Perfecting a dog's honoring is not difficult if you are firm and consistent. The result is very rewarding.

CORRECTING THE FALSE POINTER

The dog that points lesser game or ground scent left by birds that have long since departed must be taught to discriminate between what the handler considers worthy of pointing and what is not. If it is lesser birds, indifference by the handler by riding or walking by when it is obvious that the dog is not on the real thing should soon persuade him to ignore the lesser scents.

Keeping the dog moving with a high head will, of course, encourage performance by body scent rather than foot or ground scent and eliminate other than body-scent pointing.

We must recognize that overemphasis on some phases of training encourages overcaution and may lead to false pointing.

The most amusing false pointer I ever witnessed involves a story and a lesson worth telling. A well-known handler of a breed of pointing dogs not reputed for their range produced a dog that ran surprisingly wide, albeit he never located game under my judging until he had dropped to a trot or walk. The dog's success because of his range evidently encouraged the trainer to endeavor to ride another dog out into the same big pattern (the dog had obviously been driven wide). Time came in a trial with hour heats when the weather was hot and dry. When the dog had been out long

The Vizsla is a proficient and eager hunter of waterfowl as well as of upland game.

The German Shorthaired Pointer has figured prominently on the American hunting scene since his arrival.

enough to feel the strain he suddenly pointed, but on a piece of completely bare ground. The handler called point and dismounted to flush the bird, though it would have to have been from a hole in the ground. There was obviously no bird. The dog was sent on and ridden out, but suddenly pointed again on an equally unlikely spot. This happened until the handler, completely embassassed and the secret of his methods unquestionably exposed, threw in the towel and picked up the dog.

THE CURE FOR BUMPING

If a dog only bumps birds occasionally, it may be a reasonable average considering the conditions under which he is working. Bumping is more likely going down wind. After a covey flush, singles keep their feathers tight and do not move around, so they give off relatively little scent. Consistent bumping may be the result of poor nose, which may be temporary because of illness or a permanent defect in the dog's scenting powers. If you determine that it is intentional, it is then necessary to stop the dog on each occasion, return him to the place where he transgressed, and set him up on point. If he persists, and you are positive that his nose knows better, chastisement is in order, as a dog which purposely and persistently bumps birds is an abomination.

9. The Hunt

FINISHED CONTROL

Bursting through kennel doors, boisterous entry into house or elevator, pushing in or out of car doors—all involve a kind of control that can make the difference between pleasure and aggravation or even disaster in handling a dog, especially if it travels under varying circumstances. Even casting a dog off for a day's hunt or a field trial heat can be done with far more satisfaction if the dog has the finish and response of a perfect canine gentleman.

Consistency must be practiced in order to accomplish this. The satisfaction and convenience gained is ample reward for the effort. Command

Bobo Grabenbruch, a German Shorthaired Pointer, winning an important field trial. Field trials have become very popular over the past few years.

A dog that has been taught to be steady to wing and shot will always make a more reliable hunting companion.

the dog to stand, or whoa, at doors, elevators, and car doors, and make sure that he does. Do not allow him to proceed until you have told him he may. The command *"all right"* fits the situation well, since the command can be generally used as a go ahead signal, a release from restricting commands. Casting a dog at a field trial is much more impressive if the dog stands obediently, though impatient to get started, until the signal. The traditional field trial signal is two short whistle blasts as used to send or encourage a dog on from anywhere in the hunting field. Associated with the *"all right"* command, a dog that is working with you will make this transfer quickly.

IDEAL SHOOTING DOG

Only a few of us can be blessed with dogs that come close to the ideal. That is no reason, however, why we should not recognize the qualities expected in top performers and direct our energies toward doing the best possible with such dogs as we have or are able to obtain. With this in mind, let's consider what characteristics a top pointing dog should have.

I like to use the automobile as an analogy in describing ability versus handling, and I find the same requirements essential. A really great dog, like a great car, should be capable of speed with stamina, but both must have the brakes and steering to maintain good control at all times, and both should be smoothly maneuverable at slow speeds when desired. Either a dog or a car which can go but cannot be controlled is useless. A slow dog or car which gets the job done safely and effectively, though not spectacularly, is serviceable and worthy of respect. Both are good, though they may not be great.

Desirable qualities in a pointing dog are an easy, ground-covering gait, desire to use it to reach likely objectives, a sense of which objectives are likely, and a nose to recognize and locate game when it is approached. The instinct to point is necessary as is the intensity that will make the point look good and incline the dog to remain on point until arrival of the gun. Temperament must be such as will enable the trainer to steady the dog to wing and shot while retaining loftiness and spirit and to train him to hunt to the gun and to honor another dog's work. Should retrieving be required,

The Texas Traveler, one of the most famous of field trial Pointers, in a classic study. The dog's expression reflects the intensity which the Pointer applies in the field. Photo by R. H. Hicks.

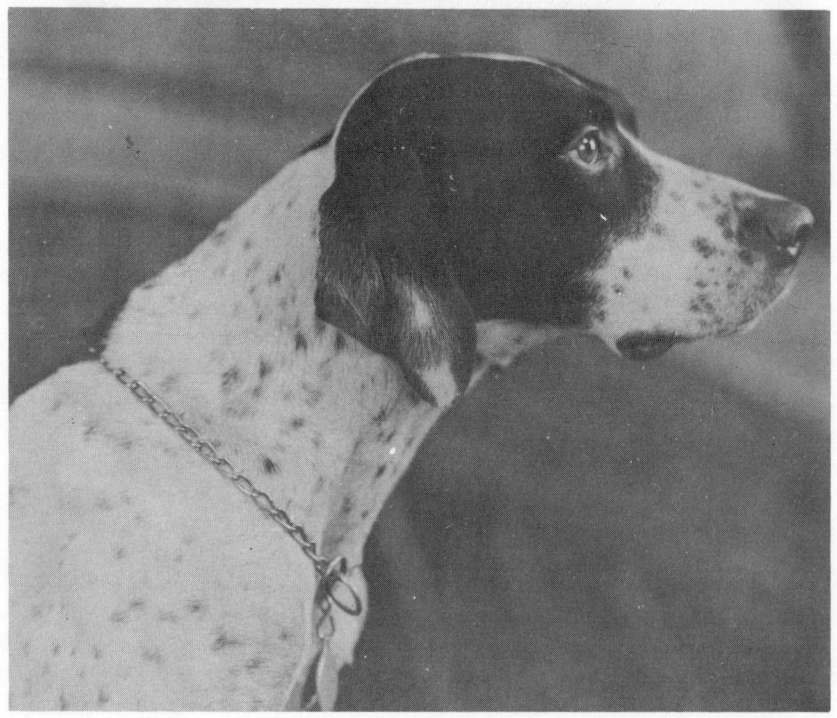

The Pudel Pointers pictured above and below are great favorites among European hunters. They are not widely known in the United States.

This English Setter has located and is pointing birds; his handler is flushing them for a shot.

there must be marking ability, which includes good sight with depth, perception and memory, a good pick-up, soft mouth, and clean delivery. Needless to say, the dog cannot be gunshy and will be much easier to live with if he is of a nature that can get along with people and other dogs. If he is good looking as well, "our cup runneth over."

COURTESY IN THE FIELD

The responsibilities of the owner of a pointing dog to other hunters and their dogs are particularly important, since an unmannerly, or uncontrolled, dog, or one which may be quite teachable and cooperative but breaks on flush or shot, can not only reduce the pleasure of a day's shooting but also interferes with the work of other dogs. The most beautifully finished dog will find it difficult to hold a point or remain steady while an undisciplined dog sneaks in front of his point, flushes the bird out from under his point, or breaks and chases on flush. The youth of a dog may be an excuse for his lack of training, but it is no excuse for inflicting the rollicking infant on the other hunter and his dog.

When permission has been granted, (and make sure it is really meant) a young dog may gain considerable valuable experience by working with a veteran, but care should be taken to prevent the young dog from interfering with the other dog's work. If the veteran points, efforts should be made to get the youngster to back. If he will not back on sight or command, get a line on him, bring him up to backing position and use the opportunity as a lesson. Naturally he should be kept in check on the flush.

Even a youngster that will show initiative and interest in likely objectives when working alone may tag on to another dog and trail. He should be picked up and cast off in another area. If he persists, pick him up permanently.

One cardinal sin is handling another man's dog in the field. There may be exceptions to this, of course, especially if the handler is not present and his dog gets into trouble, but, generally speaking, leave the handling of a dog to its owner.

If you intend taking your dog in another man's car, be sure the dog is clean and well groomed. It is a bit too much to take a dirty, smelly dog, with shedding hair, into a car that may have to be used for business or as the family conveyance.

The Vizsla, or Hungarian Pointer, is the newest recognized sporting breed in the United States. He is quickly proving himself as useful in the field as some of his better known cousins.

These pictures illustrate a continental hunting method called **Bringsel**. The dog, a German Wirehaired Pointer, is put on line in this demonstration. He locates the deerskin. On locating the skin he mouths a short stick (the bat) which is tied to his collar. He now returns to the hunter with the bat or **bringsel** in his mouth. The dog is expected to keep the bat in his mouth through any kind of cover. When he returns to the hunter with the bat in his mouth, the hunter knows the dog has located the game and then lets the dog lead him to it. The comparison of European and American hunting methods make an interesting topic for the sportsman's study.

The pleasures of hunting over a good pointing dog are many. The dog can bring trophies for the den, meat for the table and endless hours of enjoyment for the sportsman.

MALE OR FEMALE

The question often arises as to which sex is superior for hunting. There are strong proponents for both, but the question usually comes down to the greater difficulty encountered with bitches because of their seasons. If a bitch comes in season out of the hunting season, there is no concern more than the usual precautionary measures involved. It is when she schedules her matronly differences for hunting time that the real problem arises. Today, however, we need not be inconvenienced by this since your veterinarian can prescribe treatment which will delay her indisposition until hunting season is over. This will in no way concern the hunter not interested in a breeding program and should be of little concern to the breeder if the delay is of a short duration. A long delay should not be necessary if scheduling is properly predicted, since hunting seasons are no longer of appreciable duration.

Regarding pertinent characteristics otherwise, it is my impression that bitches are usually easier to break, less likely to be hard-headed, readily carry capably, and are more bird-wise when given similar experience.

This nine-week-old English Setter puppy pauses for a moment while quartering a field. The sportsman who gets this puppy will be very fortunate to have such a promising gun dog.

SELF HUNTING

Dogs allowed to go about without restriction will often hunt on their own. Obviously such dogs can get into all kinds of trouble. It is possible they may wind up as chicken or sheep killers if there is livestock in the area. They can develop their own hunting habits and will likely break any training they have acquired. They will also have less initiative when taken afield by the hunter, since their independent hunting has satisfied their desire to find game. They have a ball on their own. Why should they get excited about working under discipline?

What can be done about this fault?

This type of thing can be avoided altogether by proper supervision and preventing the dog from roaming. A kennel or run is best for accomplishing this.

10. Some Final Thoughts

HUNTING DOGS AS PETS

A frequently asked question is whether a dog intended for hunting should be accepted and treated as a house pet. My answer to this is given with a definite reservation. First let me say that there have been top field dogs that were house pets. The famous pointer "Texas Traveler" was one. The last setter to win the National Bird Dog Championship, "Mississippi Zev," was taken into the home by his trainer-handler, Earl Bufkin. In fact, it is likely that "Zev" would not have been the perfect working arm of his handler that he became were it not for the understanding established by dog and handler living together. It must be remembered, however, that Earl

This brace of English Setters, of the Ryman type, has brought in enough pheasant and grouse to keep the family larder well stocked for a long time.

Mississippi Zev, a famous English Setter, lived as a house pet in the home of his trainer. A field dog can be kept as a pet provided all in the household are consistent in their commands to him.

knew what he was doing in his every relationship with the dog. There were no inconsistencies to cause confusion. There were no commands given unnecessarily, and when a command was given it was followed to the proper conclusion. Whether a dog will retain its hunting enthusiasm and its response to training depends upon the temperament of the dog and the ability of members of the household to respect the dog's dignity, training, and response.

CONCLUSION

There comes that frosty morning with the crisp leaves underfoot, the grasses brittle, and the weed seeds using every least excuse to scatter in the breeze. Later in the day the skies may shed a bit of snow or an Indian summer sun may filter through the canopy of branches, whose last quivering leaves rustle a warning of impending winter winds.

The air is pregnant with anticipation of the hunt. It's opening day and at your side, restrained but straining as on springs of steel, the dog you've molded to your hunting needs is fit and eager to perform and waits but for your signal to be off.

A point and a back executed by two skillful English Setters. Their owners enjoy hunting over them because the dogs were carefully trained to this level of perfection in the field.

The partnership of a man and his bird dog is one of the oldest and most enduring combinations in the world of sport. A good dog, well trained, is a constant source of pride to his owner. Photo courtesy of Field & Stream.

You leave the dirt road, climb the wall into the orchard, slip two shells into your broken gun and swing the barrels into place; then, with the tingle that the oldest veteran can't deny, you cast the bunch of quivering muscles off along the hedgerow to the left.

Using the moving in to best advantage he slips through the cover and races down the lee side, taking the stone wall at the far end in stride, and swings still further left, downwind, into the bracken of a fallow field. Just when hopes are high a bird gets up, towers, and slides down the wind. Has all the training gone for naught? Is the season to be spent bumping birds out of gunshot? *"Whoa,"* you yell, perhaps a bit too loudly and perhaps with reprimand and anger in your voice, seeking an opening through which to see. And there he stands anxious and aquiver waiting your approach. Yes, he's been traveling too fast for his nose on this chill morning. It was downwind and he got in too close. But you can be proud. With all his urge to go and with a bird in the air in front of him, he responded to training. He stopped to flush. Of all the pointing, steadiness to wing and shot, backing and retrieving you've experienced with him in training you need have no fear. He's passed the acid test. You have a finished pointing dog.

Recommended Reading

Breed Your Dog, Dr. Leon Whitney, 64 pp., $1.00. Illustrated throughout with instructive photographs in both color and black and white. Covers aspects of breeding through puppyhood.

Dollars In Dogs, Leon F. Whitney, D.V.M., 255 pp., $4.95. Twenty-six chapters on different vocations in the vast field of dog business. An excellent book for your library.

First Aid For Your Dog, Dr. Herbert Richards, 64 pp., $1.00. Illustrated throughout in both color and black and white.

Groom Your Dog, Leon F. Whitney, D.V.M., 64 pp., $1.00. Illustrated throughout with both color and black and white photographs showing various grooming techniques.

How To Feed Your Dog, Dr. Leon F. Whitney, 64 pp., $1.00. Best diets and feeding routines for puppies and adult canines. Profusely illustrated in color and black and white.

How To Housebreak And Train Your Dog, Arthur Liebers, 80 pp., $1.00. Six educational chapters on training your dog. Illustrated in color and black and white photographs.

How To Raise And Train A Pedigreed Or Mixed Breed Puppy, Arthur Liebers, 64 pp., $1.00. Nine chapters covering such canine questions as choosing your puppy through breeding the adult. Illustrated in both color and black and white photographs.

How To Show Your Dog, Virginia Tuck Nichols, 252 pp., $4.95. This book is written for the novice who plans to show his dog. An excellent text to make your dog library complete.

The Distemper Complex, Leon F. Whitney, D.V.M., and George D. Whitney, D.V.M., 219 pp., $5.00. A comprehensive canine health book. Nineteen revealing chapters. A thirty-nine-page bibliography. Completely indexed.

This Is The Puppy, Ernest Hart, 190 pp., $4.95. Eleven profusely-illustrated chapters to guide the reader in the care and selection of a puppy. Full-color photographs. Also black and white candids. Indexed.